DELIGHT IN THE FATHER OF GLORY

Bible Study
Designed for Discipleship

GABRIELE GILPIN

DELIGHT IN THE FATHER OF GLORY

DELIGHT ~

TO LOVE SOMEONE GREATLY; TO BE FASCINATED, CAPTIVATED AND ATTRACTED

ISBN: 0692528423
ISBN-13: 978-0692528426 (Custom)

Soaring Eagle Ministries, Inc.
10990 Ft. Caroline Road # 350352
Jacksonville, FL 32225
Visit us online: www.soaringeagleinc.org

Printed in the United States of America.

Unless otherwise indicated, all Scriptures taken from the New King James Version. Other versions are abbreviated as follows: NLT (New Living Translation), GNT (Good News Translation and AMP (Amplified Bible), (NIV) New International Version

HOW TO USE THIS MATERIAL

The goal of this booklet is not to teach a lesson but to apply truth to our lives. It is designed for individual or group discipleship and discussion. When Jesus called His disciples, He gave a brief invitation and then turned and started to walk away. After His invitation it was up to the "called out ones" to follow Him, actually delighting in taking up their cross daily (see Luke 9:23).

My expectation is that this booklet will be a launching pad into new adventures and journeys with the Father; changing and transforming you forever! I encourage you to partner with someone else, or do this together as a church, home group or youth group.

Following are some suggestions on how to use this booklet:

Warm-up

Focus on Thanksgiving – Our Heavenly Father hears, responds and delights in you! How can we not give thanks?! Spend some time to thank Him – thanking Him for life, Jesus, friendships, loved ones, salvation, love, laughter and so on...

1 Thessalonians 5:18, Psalm 50:14, 15, Psalm 100:4, Psalm 57:7, Psalm 95:2

Focus on Praise – The greatness and magnificence of God
John 4:23-24, Exodus 15:11, Psalm 8, Revelation 5:8-10

Focus on Worship – When we worship in Spirit and Truth, we get lost in His Presence and Glory!
Psalm 29:2, Psalm 49:9, Revelation 4:1-11

Word

Each lesson has several key points in bold type followed by scripture, brief comments, questions, and some blank space. The questions are there to help you share and communicate your insight. Use the blank space to record additional comments, illustrations, and thoughts.

Personal Application

The goal is to "Delight in the Father of Glory", to learn more about Him, to dive into His mysteries and to apply the truth revealed to us. Personal application is at the very heart of discipleship and spiritual growth.

Receive the "good news" of God's kingdom and enjoy the journey with Him, imitating the Father and remaining free in Christ Jesus. Jesus said in John 6:63: "It is the Spirit who gives life; the flesh profits nothing. The words that I speak to you are spirit, and they are life."

As ambassadors of Christ, we have been translated out of darkness and into His marvelous light and we are called to be the light of the world and the salt of the earth. There is no need to strive and labor to become good enough to receive His love, forgiveness, and intimacy. Whether you believe it or not, you are already positional seated with Him in heavenly places and you can grow up becoming mature sons and daughters.

Journaling/Personal Notes

A journal is a written record of thoughts, prayers, inspirations, experiences, dreams, observations and revelations. Journaling can be done daily, or only whenever inspired. A leather-bound book, a notebook, a composition booklet or any other means of record keeping can be used to pen down important prompts. It's entirely up to the one journaling.

Personally, I have journaled for decades and it has been a wonderful inspiration to go back reading and remembering revelations and strategies in the word of God as given by the Holy Spirit, personal prophecies, answers to prayer and other exciting things. As well as heartfelt situations I was blessed to walk through and overcome.

Bible journaling is a hot topic. There are many wonderful ways to read and study the Bible using journaling techniques. Some can be art and doodling techniques.

- You can highlight and write in the side margins in your handwriting, the way many readers have done it for years.
- You can use the wide-margin Bible and expand your notes to include artistic elements, either stamping, drawing or any other ways you enjoy.

Prayer

Prayer is communication with an amazing Father and Son (see 1 John 1:3).

Jesus taught His disciples to pray the Lord's Prayer (see Matthew 6:9-13), Jude talked about praying in the Holy Spirit to "build ourselves up on our most Holy faith" (see Jude 20) and Paul talked about praying in "tongues more than you all" (see 1 Corinthians 14:18).

Prayer is a conversation not a ritual and it is meant to be enjoyed. We can rely on the Holy Spirit to assist us in praying the Father's perfect will, because the Spirit Himself makes intercession for us. Those that let the Spirit of God lead them are sons and daughters of God. (see Romans 8)

TABLE OF CONTENTS

DELIGHT
IN THE
FATHER OF GLORY

JOB 22:21-27 AMP

²¹ *Acquaint now yourself with Him [agree with God and show yourself to be conformed to His will] and be at peace; by that [you shall prosper and great] good shall come to you.*

²² *Receive, I pray you, the law and instruction from His mouth and lay up His words in your heart.*

²³ *If you return to the Almighty [and submit and humble yourself before Him], you will be built up; if you put away unrighteousness far from your tents,*

²⁴ *If you lay gold in the dust, and the gold of Ophir among the stones of the brook [considering them of little worth],*

²⁵ *And make the Almighty your gold and [the Lord] your precious silver treasure,*

²⁶ *Then you will have delight in the Almighty, and you will lift up your face to God.*

²⁷ *You will make your prayer to Him, and He will hear you, and you will pay your vows.*

1

God is Love

WORD

Ephesians 3:17-19

I pray that Christ may dwell in your hearts through faith; that you, being rooted and grounded in love, ¹⁸ may be able to comprehend with all the saints what is the width and length and depth and height— ¹⁹ to know the love of Christ which passes knowledge; that you may be filled with all the fullness of God.

Apostle Paul prayed that the saints, the set apart ones, would know and comprehend the magnitude of the love of Christ. It is a quest worth pursuing, in order to gain the revelation on how much the Lord truly loves us and that we can be filled to overflowing with all the fullness of God. After all, one of the central themes of the Bible is God's love for man. Let's discover this love, walk in this love and spread this love all around.

God's love is everlasting

Jeremiah 31:3

The Lord has appeared of old to me, saying: "Yes, I have loved you with an everlasting love; Therefore with lovingkindness I have drawn you.

There is no end to God's love; whereas people "fall in love" and in a few years or less, they fall out of love.

The Father has drawn us with His lovingkindness and His love is everlasting. It is like our hearts are sealed, because God's love is as strong as death and many waters cannot quench love, neither can the floods drown it (see Song of Solomon 8:6-7).

When we truly love someone, we want to know what is in their heart. There is a desire to receive more of the Father's love in His glorious presence. Let's guard the passion of devotion to the "ONE" and continue to fan the flames of your first love!

Explain the word "everlasting" in your own words and write about your first love:

God's love is great

1 John 3:1

How great is the love the Father has lavished on us, that we should be called children of God! And that is what we are!

The Father's love has been richly lavished on all his children. Isn't it amazing, that we are called the children of God? We love Him because He first loved us. Our Father started it all by loving the world so much, sending His Son Jesus Christ to be the Redeemer and Savior.

Can you share what the word "lavished" means to you?

God's love never changes

Romans 8:35-39

[35] *Who shall separate us from the love of Christ? Shall tribulation, or distress, or persecution, or famine, or nakedness, or peril, or sword?* [36] *As it is written: "For Your sake we are killed all day long; We are accounted as sheep for the slaughter.* [37] *Yet in all these things we are more than conquerors through Him who loved us.* [38] *For I am persuaded that neither death nor life, nor angels nor principalities nor powers, nor things present nor things to come,* [39] *nor height nor depth, nor any other created thing, shall be able to separate us from the love of God which is in Christ Jesus our Lord.*

The Bible promises that Jesus Christ will lead us besides still waters and that He even walks us through the valley of the shadow of death. In times of distress and suffering we have opportunities to get to know Him more intimately. We are promised that as long as we draw close to Him, He will draw close to us.

Our Father loves us at all times and we can be filled with His love and presence continuously. Nothing can ever separate us from the constant and unchanging love of God. His perfect love actually removes all fear!

3

What recent pain or trials have you undergone, in which you have found great encouragement in the perfect love of God?

God's love is unfailing

Lamentations 3:21-24 GNT

"Yet hope returns when I remember this one thing: The Lord's unfailing love and mercy still continue, fresh as the morning, as sure as the sunrise. The Lord is all I have, and so in him I put my hope."

We have a hope as an anchor for our soul, it is firm and secure, because we put our hope and trust in Jesus Christ. (see Hebrews 6:19) During times of difficulties and strange fiery trials, this hope and the Lord's unfailing love and mercy is always available. As we count it all joy and allow patience to mature, we will lack nothing and walk in God's fullness. (see James 1)

Is the Lord all you have and is He the One you run to? In what or whom do you put your hope and trust?

PERSONAL APPLICATION

Are you certain that God loves you at all times? Why?

Do you ever question God's love especially during a wilderness time, when God seems to be quiet and you are walking through the fire of adversity?

PRAYER

Record prayer requests and answers to prayer.

PERSONAL NOTES:

2

Father of Glory

WORD

Job 22:21

"Now acquaint yourself with Him, and be at peace. Thereby good will come to you."

It is important to get to know the ways the Lord operates and to grow closer to Him. The word acquaint is also translated as "agreeing with God." It is vital to agree with the Lord's purposes and understand that we are God's handiwork, created and born anew in Christ Jesus. We can enjoy the paths which He prepared ahead of time, so that we can walk in them and live the abundant, exceptional life He made ready for us (see Ephesians 2:10).

In the scripture in John 15, we are asked to "Abide in Him;" learning to practice His presence every moment of every day. It tells me that I can't do anything apart from Him, but with God all things are possible and I am deeply aware of His love as I look to Him for wisdom, guidance and understanding.

The Lord's faithful heart can be completely trusted at all times. His heart towards us is full of a Father's love and He delights in us, therefore He desires to lead us with one eye upon us at all times. His eyes are on the sparrow and His eyes are on us. He guides us as the Great Shepherd, leading us besides still waters and restoring our soul. Even during our walk through dark times, His rod brings correction if needed, but His staff directs us into a place of peace. That's why we can be at peace with what He is doing, as we live and move and have our being in Jesus and in His kingdom.

The statement: *"Thereby good will come to you,"* is an overflow of remaining close to Him, becoming deeply intertwined with Him, cherishing Him, partaking of His life and dwelling in the Secret Place of the Most High. From that position in Him, as the Father of Creativity, everything else will flow as He enables us to fulfill the things He called us to. He is unlocking creativity and the talents within us making all things beautiful in His perfect timing.

Jesus came not to condemn us but to set us FREE and to give us abundant life! (John 10:10)

Have you partaken of the abundant life Jesus provided? Have you been abiding in Him? Write your answer below.

What does it mean to you to trust in the Father's faithful heart no matter what?

Insight into mysteries and secrets in the deep and intimate knowledge of Him

Another Bible verse that comes to mind is in Ephesians 1:17. Apostle Paul is praying:

Ephesians 1:17 Amp

[17] [For I always pray to] the God of our Lord Jesus Christ, the Father of glory, that He may grant you a spirit of wisdom and revelation [of insight into mysteries and secrets] in the [deep and intimate] knowledge of Him.

The spirit of wisdom and revelation will reveal strategies and insight into mysteries and secrets hidden in Jesus Christ. A song I heard recently: "We will see the look on Your Face, we will hear the tone of Your Voice, and we will change as we behold You," pierced my heart and reminded me to draw closer to the Father and to behold Him. Those moments set apart for Him only, the looks and gazes we share are for His eyes only and I am transformed forever, because of looking toward the One, whose voice is that of my Shepherd and I can see the Father's majestic reflection in Jesus' face.

The precious Holy Spirit will be the One, who helps us, comforts us and comes along side of us in this quest for more understanding and depth in a true knowledge of God's mystery. It is time to search for the deep things of God and to seek His kingdom and His righteousness first.

Colossians 2:2-3

2 that their hearts may be encouraged, having been knit together in love, and attaining to all the wealth that comes from the full assurance of understanding, resulting in a true knowledge of God's mystery, that is, Christ Himself, 3 in whom are hidden all the treasures of wisdom and knowledge....

We truly have this treasure in earthen vessels that the excellency of the power may be of God flowing through us. Remember when you see Jesus, you also see the Father.

Have you received fresh insight from the Lord? What does that look like and what kind of impact does it have on you?

Consider this… Christ in you is the hope of glory! Read the following scriptures and pray for revelation knowledge from the Lord.

Colossians 1:26-28

26 the mystery which has been hidden from ages and from generations, but now has been revealed to His saints. 27 To them God willed to make known what are the riches of the glory of this mystery among the Gentiles: which is **Christ in you, the hope of glory.** *28 Him we preach, warning every man and teaching every man in all wisdom, that we may present every man perfect in Christ Jesus.*

2 Thessalonians 1:10-12

¹⁰ when He comes, in that Day, to be glorified in His saints and to be admired among all those who believe, because our testimony among you was believed. ¹¹ Therefore we also pray always for you that our God would count you worthy of this calling, and fulfill all the good pleasure of His goodness and the work of faith with power, ¹² that the name of our Lord Jesus Christ may be glorified in you, and you in Him, according to the grace of our God and the Lord Jesus Christ.

The Eyes of Our Heart

Ephesians 1:18 Amp

18 By having the eyes of your heart flooded with light, so that you can know and understand the hope to which He has called you, and how rich is His glorious inheritance in the saints (His set-apart ones)

Our eyes need to be flooded with light, which represents fresh perception, illumination and revelation. The Lord has revealed things which He has prepared for those who love Him by and through the Holy Spirit. We can and need to know the hope to which He has called us, and to understand how rich His glorious inheritance is for His set-apart ones. We have the opportunity to see and hear heavenly things that God has fashioned for those who love Him. *Oh, the depth and the riches both of the wisdom and knowledge of God available to us!*

1 Corinthians 2:9-12

But as it is written: "Eye has not seen, nor ear heard, nor have entered into the heart of man the things which God has prepared for those who love Him." 10 But God has revealed them to us through His Spirit. For the Spirit searches all things, yes, the deep things of God. 11 For what man knows the things of a man except the spirit of the man which is in him? Even so no one knows the things of God except the Spirit of God. 12 Now we have received, not the spirit of the world, but the Spirit who is from God, that we might know the things that have been freely given to us by God.

Have you prayed for the spirit of wisdom and revelation to give you understanding of the deep things of God?

Seated in Heavenly Places together with Him

Ephesians 2:6 Amp

6 And He raised us up together with Him and made us sit down together [giving us joint seating with Him] in the heavenly sphere [by virtue of our being] in Christ Jesus (the Messiah, the Anointed One).

We are exhorted to humble ourselves under the mighty hand of God and in due time, He will raise us up, because He gives grace to the humble while resisting the proud. God is offering grace to go higher as we respectfully posture ourselves at the feet of Jesus.

Spending time at Jesus' feet includes knowing our position in Christ. We have been raised up together with Christ and made to sit "in heavenly places" indicating a position of authority, which means that all things, including the demonic realm, are put under our feet (Ephesians 1:22-23). We are authorized to exercise this authority in the present age through preaching the Gospel, including healing the sick and casting out devils, declaring and decreeing His Word and releasing Kingdom of God manifestations. (Matthew 10:7-8)

After this I looked, and, behold, a door was opened in heaven: and the first voice which I heard was as it were of a trumpet talking with me; which said, Come up here, and I will show you things which must be hereafter (see Revelations 4:1).

Since we are resurrected with Jesus and seated with Him in heavenly places, what is true of Him is also true of us in our born-again spirits. We not only can do the same works that Jesus did, but even greater works shall we do, because He has gone to be with His Father (see John 14:12).

Have you understood the authority you can exercise as a born-again believer seated with Jesus in heavenly places?

What are your thoughts on the fact that Jesus Christ is the door to enter into the heavenly realm? (John 10:7, Rev. 4:1)

PERSONAL APPLICATION

CONSIDER THIS: As a son or daughter of God, we have unlimited access to getting to know Him and to receiving His healing, love and encouragement to give to others. Anything we have received from the Father can be given away freely to others. *"Freely you have received, freely give" (see Matthew 10:8).* Share your thoughts:

PRAYER

Pray, speak and sing in the Spirit. Allow your spirit to pray and intercede in various ways, from tongues to worshipful melodies, to praying in a known language.

But you, beloved, building yourselves up on your most holy faith, praying in the Holy Spirit. (Jude 20)

PERSONAL NOTES:

3

Receive Instruction

WORD

Job 22:22

"Receive, please, instruction from His mouth and lay up His words in your heart."

How important is it to receive the Lord's instruction?

This reminds me of the time Jesus spent in the wilderness being tempted by the devil (see Matthew 4). When the devil tried to entice Jesus to turn the stones into bread, Jesus replied by quoting the Word of God.

The Father still speaks

Matthew 4:4 AMP

[4] *But He replied, It has been written, Man shall not live and be upheld and sustained by bread alone, but by every word that comes forth from the mouth of God.*

We have the Bible as the written word of God, but that is not all, because the Father still speaks to us and releases strategies and instruction for our daily lives. When I travel the nations, I don't just go anywhere I please, but I wait upon the Lord to give me direction and His perfect timing to where I am send. I have not found a book in the Bible with my name on it giving me personal directions, for instance: "Gabriele I am sending you to Cyprus in April to preach the Good News of the Kingdom of God." This can't be found in the Bible, but I can read in Isaiah 6: "Who will go for us?" and Isaiah replies: "Here I am send me." I received my call to the nations through this scripture and now I am open to prophetic revelation of the Lord's specific guidance in my live and ministry.

The Lord has given guidance in various ways; by His Word, by prophecy, by dreams, visions, signs and messenger angels.

Following are examples on how the Apostles received directions:

~ Apostle Peter received directions through a vision while praying on a rooftop (*Acts 10:9-48*).

 ~ An angel tells the Apostle Paul that he and those with him on the ship will not lose their lives at sea (*Acts 27:1-2, 21-25*).

~ And the Lord said to Paul in a vision, "Do not be afraid, but go on speaking and do not be silent" (*Acts 18:9*).

How and when has the Lord given personal direction to you?

Remember we do not live by physical food alone, but we also need a fresh word from the Living Bread, Jesus, every day to sustain us spiritually, to restore our soul and for the Holy Spirit to quicken our physical body.

The Instructions of the Lord are Perfect

Psalm 19:7 NLT

The instructions of the Lord are perfect, reviving the soul. The decrees of the Lord are trustworthy, making wise the simple.

Psalm 32:8

I will instruct you and teach you in the way you should go. I will guide you with My eye

It is a very intimate gesture when someone guides you with the eye. Growing up I always knew my mother's instruction from her looks. She would look at me a certain way and I received instruction from her gaze. No need to ask any questions, because I knew what was asked of me.

The Lord's instruction is designed to restore and refresh our soul. He provides wisdom for every decision we have to make and He gives direction and strategies in times of trouble and need.

Have you asked the Lord for wisdom and instruction while making decisions? Share about receiving instruction and the outcome.

.

Lay Up and Hide His Words In Your Heart

Psalm 119: 10–12

10 With my whole heart I have sought You; Oh, let me not wander from Your commandments! 11 Your word I have hidden in my heart, That I might not sin against You. 12 Blessed are You, O Lord! Teach me Your statutes.

Psalm 1:1-2 NIV

Blessed is the one…whose delight is in the law of the Lord, and who meditates on his law (God's words in the Bible) day and night.

Joshua 1:8

This Book of the Law shall not depart from your mouth, but you shall meditate in it day and night, that you may observe to do according to all that is written in it. For then you will make your way prosperous, and then you will have good success.

Throughout my day, I may hear a scripture in my heart. Sometimes it is to warn me from imminent danger, while other times it is for my encouragement or for guidance. But it is always God-breathed and brings the above scripture to live. I have hidden and laid up God's word in my heart throughout decades. It is never in vain to read the word and meditate on it. To mediate on scriptures means to reflect upon and to contemplate or think about it. Meditating will cause scripture to "dwell in us" and to come alive, because they are living words (See Hebrews 4:12).

Personally, I like to hold scriptures in my heart as I linger in His presence. Considering God's word stirs a hunger in me for the Lord and all He has said and done. Jesus taught in John 6:63: *"It is the Spirit who gives life; the flesh profits nothing. The words that I speak to you are spirit, and they are life."*

Therefore, we can believe for an impartation of His abundant life and spirit to burn deep within us as we are absorbing the revelation of His Word in our hearts.

Seeking Him with my whole heart causes me to get closer to Jesus and sometimes I find myself being a part of the parables, He spoke of. It all becomes real to me and I receive fresh revelation. It is true that we prosper and are successful when we follow His promptings through His living word.

Allow me to explain, in a vision I saw a very long hallway with pictures on either side. When I started to walk along this hallway and turned to one of those pictures, looking intently at it, the picture would suddenly come alive. The scene out of the Bible started to turn into a movie, for instance Jesus feeding the 5,000 or Jesus being baptized by John the Baptist. Not only was I able to watch the movie, but I also became part of it, much like a spectator, who was able to smell and sense everything going on around including the culture of the time. Such a experience is what we can have by visualizing scripture, because it can help make your Bible reading more real and personal. It involves reading a passage, asking the Holy Spirit to help you picturing the details in your mind, and picturing how you personally fit into the scene.

How alive is the Word of God to you and in you? Have you pictured how, by faith; you can turn to God in the middle of such a scene receiving His help and strength?

Transformation through Renewing of the Mind

Romans 12: 1-2

I beseech you therefore, brethren, by the mercies of God, that you present your bodies a living sacrifice, holy, acceptable to God, which is your reasonable service. ²And do not be conformed to this world, but be transformed by the renewing of your mind, that you may prove what is that good and acceptable and perfect will of God.

It is super important to renew our minds daily by the washing of the water of the Word. The Living Word of God brings transformation from the inside out. The Bible tells us that we are and have what we say. Before anything comes out of our mouth, we have already thought about it. Many have strongholds in their mind and it consists of negative thinking and thoughts that are contrary to what Jesus teaches. This can be changed. Change comes when we renew the way we think, because then we see things from God's perspective. Furthermore, it is vital to guard our hearts, because out of it flows the wellspring of live. (see Proverbs 4:23)

2 Corinthians 10:5b NIV

We take captive (bring under control) every thought to make it obedient to Christ.

As we hear the Word and renew our mind daily, we will soon detect that our own thoughts are not lining up nor agreeing with what the Lord is saying. Those ungodly thoughts can be strongholds, literally representing mighty fortresses, because they have been there for a long time and are lies we have heard and believed. Now it is up to us to captivate them and tear them down and bringing those toxic thoughts to Jesus. All along feeding ourselves with the Truth to replace those undesirable thoughts and therefore renewing our mind with thoughts that are pleasing to the Lord. Jesus tells us to abide in His teaching, which simply means we are to remain in Him.

John 8:31

"If you abide in my word, you are truly my disciples."

Agreement with and abiding in His word is vital for an overcoming life in Christ. We can't be double-minded, because as the book of James tells us, we will receive nothing from the Lord if we are in confusion.

Jesus promised to teach us and therefore we can know the perfect and acceptable will of the Father. As we present our bodies a living sacrifice, we will not be conformed to this world system, but we will be transformed from the inside out.

According to 2 Corinthians 10:5b, what are you able to do with thoughts not lining up with God's truth?

Are you coming to Jesus to be loved and taught?

Have you understood how important it is to renew your mind? Have you experienced any transformation in your life?

CONSIDER THIS: In order to change our mind successfully we can intentionally renew our thought patterns and life out of the mind of Christ. It is much like: *"Out with the old and in with the new".*

1 Corinthians 2:9-10

But as it is written: "Eye has not seen, nor ear heard, Nor have entered into the   heart of man The things which God has prepared for those who love Him." 10 But God has revealed them to us through His Spirit. For the Spirit searches all things, yes, the deep things of God.

PERSONAL APPLICATION

Focus on Waiting, Listening and Silence: The Father still speaks and you can hide His word in your heart. What does the Father want to say to you?

Isaiah 40: 31, Psalm 27:14, Psalm 46:10

PRAYER

Pray for God-given dreams, visions and revelation.

Joel 2:28-29

Record prayer requests and answers to prayer.

PERSONAL NOTES:

4

Being Built Up

WORD

Job 22:23

If you return to the Almighty, you will be built up; You will remove iniquity far from your tents.

Psalm 139:23-24

Search me, O God, and know my heart; Try me, and know my anxieties; 24 And see if there is any wicked way in me, And lead me in the way everlasting.

2 Corinthians 13:5

Examine yourselves as to whether you are in the faith. Test yourselves. Do you not know yourselves, that Jesus Christ is in you?—unless indeed you are disqualified.

What is our strongest protection against our enemy? Our identity in Christ – a people loved and chosen by God, created to glorify Him and for His purposes. Living a life close to the heart of the Father keeps us as living stones, which are being built up a spiritual house and a holy priesthood. We offer up spiritual sacrifices acceptable to God through Jesus Christ. *(see 1 Peter 2:5)*

It's time to turn completely to God realizing that our bodies are the temple of the Holy Spirit. Learning to walk in the Spirit and see the fruit of the Spirit ripen daily. Endeavoring to love even the unlovable, to be joyful and at peace. Patience is developed along with all the other fruit of the Spirit listed in Galatians 5:22-23.

The Holy Spirit will search our hearts as we examine ourselves to see whether we are actually living by faith. We receive a cleansing as sin and iniquity is exposed by the light of Jesus Christ. He loves us so deeply and therefore corrects us as His dear children. We can overcome and reign in life by the abundance of grace and the gift of righteousness provided for us.

A lover of Christ does not have to live a life of constant oppression, depression, and hopelessness.

Romans 5:14-17 Nevertheless death reigned from Adam until Moses, even over those who had not sinned in the likeness of the offense of Adam, who is a type of Him who was to come. 15 But the free gift is not like the transgression. For if by the transgression of the one the many died, much more did the grace of God and the gift by the grace of the one Man, Jesus Christ, abound to the many. 16 The gift is not like that which came through the one who sinned; for on the one hand the judgment arose from one transgression resulting in condemnation, but on the other hand the free gift arose from many transgressions resulting in justification. 17 For if by the one man's offense death reigned through the one, much more those who receive abundance of grace and of the gift of righteousness will reign in life through the One, Jesus Christ.

Adam's offense caused death to all of us. But because God has given abundance of grace through the death and resurrection of Jesus Christ, we can reign over whatever adverse circumstances come our way. We can live victorious and overcoming lives in Christ, because of the free gift of the grace of God resulting in justification. We do not have to live in guilt and shame, but can thrive in life through the cleansing of the precious blood of Jesus Christ.

Built up a Spiritual House

Colossians 2:6-7

As you therefore have received Christ Jesus the Lord, so walk in Him, 7 rooted and built up in Him and established in the faith, as you have been taught, abounding in it with thanksgiving.

1 Peter 2:5

you also, as living stones, are being built up a spiritual house, a holy priesthood, to offer up spiritual sacrifices acceptable to God through Jesus Christ.

Those in Christ have a peace that transcends all things, a hope that is an anchor for the soul, a love that knows no boundary, an unquenchable joy, a message needed by those who've never heard.

Each believer is described as a Living Stone and all of us together in the Body of Christ are fitly joined and we are built up into a spiritual house for God's glory. In the book of Revelation (Revelation 1:6, 5:10, 20:6) Christians individually are called priests and the Church collectively is called a priesthood.

As a holy priesthood we come to the Lord in worship and adoration and stand before Him to give our bodies as a living sacrifice. All this is made possible by the death and resurrection of Jesus Christ. Through Him we are the righteousness of God and we can live a holy life, because all iniquity has been removed by the blood of Jesus Christ.

Furthermore, as a glorious body of Christ, His Bride, we put God's love on display! The world will see that we are His disciples, because of the love we have one for another.

What are your thoughts on being built up a spiritual house?

Built up the Body of Christ

Ephesians 4:11-16 AMP

And [His gifts to the church were varied and] He Himself appointed some as apostles [special messengers, representatives], some as prophets [who speak a new message from God to the people], some as evangelists [who spread the good news of salvation], and some as pastors and teachers [to shepherd and guide and instruct], 12 [and He did this] to fully equip and perfect the saints (God's people) for works of service, **to build up the body of Christ [the church];** *13 until we all reach oneness in the faith and in the knowledge of the Son of God, [growing spiritually] to become a mature believer, reaching to the measure of the fullness of Christ [manifesting His spiritual completeness and exercising our spiritual gifts in unity]. 14 So that we are no longer* *children [spiritually immature], tossed back and forth [like ships on a stormy sea] and carried about by every wind of [shifting] doctrine, by the cunning and trickery of [unscrupulous] men, by the deceitful scheming of people ready to do anything [for personal profit]. 15 But speaking the truth in love [in all things—both our speech and our lives expressing His truth], let us grow up in all things into Him [following His example] who is the Head—Christ. 16 From Him the whole body [the church, in all its various parts], joined and knitted firmly together by what every joint supplies, when each part is working properly, causes the body to grow and mature, **building itself up in [unselfish] love.***

Jesus gave gifts to His body, the church, when He ascended into heaven after He showed Himself to His disciples teaching them about the kingdom of God. (see Acts 1)

There are gifts of the Holy Spirit outlined in 1 Corinthians 12 and Motivational gifts in Romans 12, but the gifts referred to here are those outlined in Ephesians 4 and are the Apostles, Prophets, Evangelists, Pastors and Teachers, who are equipping and training the saints to do the work of the ministry. Those are going to be teaching and equipping until all the saints mature, reach an oneness in the faith and in the knowledge of the Son of God. Then we will no longer be like gullible children, but we will be fitly joined and supplying each other what is needed to building each other up in and through God's perfect love.

In your own words describe what Ephesians 4:11-16 is conveying.

Being built up in our most Holy Faith

Jude 1:20-21 AMP

But you, beloved, build yourselves up on [the foundation of] your most holy faith [continually progress, rise like an edifice higher and higher], pray in the Holy Spirit, 21 and keep yourselves in the love of God, waiting anxiously and looking forward to the mercy of our Lord Jesus Christ [which will bring you] to eternal life.

Praying in the Holy Spirit is one of the keys to being built up in our faith and becoming stronger in believing God's word, direction and instruction. It is vital to remain in, and to even going deeper into God's unfailing, unending and perfect love. We can, just as Jesus did, live to glorify God in an unbroken relationship and fulfil His purposes since we are already living in eternal life.

Have you had any experiences in building up your faith by praying in the Holy Spirit?
Have you encountered God's unfailing and perfect love?

Overcoming weakness through Grace

2 Corinthians 12:9

And He said to me, "My grace is sufficient for you, for My strength is made perfect in weakness." Therefore most gladly I will rather boast in my infirmities, that the power of Christ may rest upon me.

Apostle Paul was given extraordinary revelations from God. To keep him from thinking he was better than anyone else, Paul was given a thorn in the flesh. It was a messenger from Satan to torment and harass him. He asked the Lord three times to take it away. But Jesus said to him: "My grace, lovingkindness and mercy are more than enough and are always available, regardless of the situation. My power shows itself most effectively in your weakness." Paul realized when he endured hardship for the sake of Christ and his human strength failed him, then he was strong and powerful by drawing from God's strength. (see 2 Corinthians 12:7-10)

What are your weaknesses? How has His grace been sufficient? What does "sufficient" mean?

Victory over sin through Grace

Romans 6:14

For sin shall not be your masters, because you are not under law but under grace.

Titus 2:11, 12

For the grace of God that brings salvation has appeared to all men. It teaches us to say "No" to ungodliness and worldly passions, and to live self-controlled, upright and godly lives in this present age.

Jesus died to end the power of sin once and for all. He lives to glorify God in an unbroken relationship. Therefore, we can consider ourselves to be dead to sin and alive to God in Christ Jesus. Don't let sin rule your body, instead give yourself to God and live in holiness and His righteousness, as people who have been raised from death to life. (see Romans 6:10-13)

What is a master? Why should sin not be our master? Who is our master?

PERSONAL APPLICATION

What is the Lord working on in your life at this time?

What aspect of His own nature is the Father teaching you at this time?

PRAYER

Jude talked about praying in the Holy Spirit to "build ourselves up on our most Holy Faith" (see Jude 20).

PERSONAL NOTES:

5

Delight in the Almighty

W O R D

Job 22:24-26

24 Then you will lay your gold in the dust, and the gold of Ophir among the stones of the brooks. 25 Yes, the Almighty will be your gold and your precious silver; 26 For then you will have your delight in the Almighty, and lift up your face to God.

Lay your Gold in the Dust

What does it mean to lay your gold in the dust? Furthermore, what does it mean to lay the gold of Ophir among the stones in the brooks? In *2 Chronicles 1:15 it states: Also the king made silver and gold as common in Jerusalem as stones, and he made cedars as abundant as the sycamores which are in the lowland.*

This scripture tells me, that silver and gold compared to King Solomon's riches were nothing more than the rocks in the brooks. Gold was as common in Jerusalem as stones.

This concept is difficult for many to comprehend in this world system, because to some worldly treasures mean everything to them. I believe the Lord is saying to lay down the gold, to relax the grip on money and to abandon any gold-plated luxury representing those things we have acquired, and to surrender all to Him. We are to understand, that what He has for us does not compare to what we try to offer up to Him. Our accomplishments shall be clearly seen for what they are, because God's Refiner's Fire will test everyone's work. It will be revealed if the efforts done have been solely driven by fleshly desires, or have been motivated and orchestrated through the Holy Spirit's leading.

1 Corinthians 3:12-15

12 Now if any man build upon this foundation gold, silver, precious stones, wood, hay, stubble; 13 Every man's work shall be made manifest: for the day shall declare it, because it shall be revealed by fire; and the fire shall try every man's work of what sort it is. 14 If anyone's work which he has built on it endures, he will receive a reward. 15 If anyone's work is burned, he will suffer loss; but he himself will be saved, yet so as through fire.

It has been said that we can have many things, but the things should not control us. Is it possible to let go of those things that keep us distracted from focusing on Jesus? What are your thoughts about being guided by the Holy Spirit into God's perfect will?

The Almighty will be your gold

Job 22:25

25 Yes, the Almighty will be your gold and your precious silver;

Revelations 3:18

I counsel you to buy from Me gold refined in the fire, that you may be rich; and white garments, that you may be clothed, that the shame of your nakedness may not be revealed; and anoint your eyes with eye salve, that you may see.

The church at Laodicea heard a stern rebuke from the angel sent to them by the Lord (Revelations 3). These people were lukewarm and were saying: "I am rich, have become wealthy, and have need of nothing – and did not know that they were wretched, miserable, poor, blind and naked! Because of their greed the Lord is counseling them to buy from Him gold refined in the fire. They were spiritually bankrupt and did not even realize the state of their supernatural blindness. But they had opportunity to turn from their wayward ways and receive eye salve from Jesus, in order to be able to see what the Holy Spirit was trying to show them. Their nakedness, which represents the exposure of the flesh not covered by His glory, could be clothed by white garments provided by the Lord. They had to overcome temptations. The Lord asked them to open the door to their heart to Him and to make Him "their gold, treasure and delight."

Have you opened your heart fully to the Lord? Have you allowed Him to love you, to show you His purpose and cover you in the areas of exposure?

The Lord is my Treasure

Matthew 6:20-21

20 but lay up for yourselves treasures in heaven, where neither moth nor rust destroys and where thieves do not break in and steal. 21 For where your treasure is, there your heart will be also.

Matthew 22:37-40

37 Jesus said to him, "'You shall love the Lord your God with all your heart, with all your soul, and with all your mind.' 38 This is the first and great commandment. 39 And the second is like it: 'You shall love your neighbor as yourself.' 40 On these two commandments hang all the Law and the Prophets."

Is the Lord, our God, our first love? Do we love Him with all our heart, soul and mind? Is the Lord our portion and our treasure to behold? Is He the pearl of great price (Matthew 13:45-46)?

In the above verses in Matthew 6, Jesus explained why one should store one's treasure in heaven rather than on earth.

Have you pondered the meaning of this teaching? Where is your Treasure?

Names and descriptions of the Father and Jesus

Psalm 9:10

Those who know your name trust in you, for you, Lord, have never forsaken those who seek you."

We can turn to the Father because of who He is and if we learn and experience God's character, we'll be more likely to trust and delight in Him. It is up to us to choose to do so. Following are some names, titles and descriptions to ponder.

Creator
Isaiah 40:28

Father
Malachi 2:10, Matthew 5:45, 6:9, John 14:6, 20:17, Romans 8:15

Father of lights
James 1:17

Father of our spirits
Hebrews 12:9

God Almighty
Genesis 17:1

God is Love
1 John 4:8

God most high
Genesis 14:18

Holy One of Israel
Isaiah 1:4

I Am
Exodus 3:14

I am the Alpha and the Omega, *the* Beginning and *the* End, the First and the Last
Revelation 1:8, Revelation 22:13

I am the Lord, I change not
Malachi 3:6

I am the Root and the Offspring of David, the Bright and Morning Star
Revelation 22:16

King of kings and Lord of lords
1 Timothy 6:15, Revelation 17:14

Light of the world
John 8:12

The Lord will provide
(Jehovah Jireh) Genesis 22:14

Savior
Isaiah 43:3

PERSONAL APPLICATION

Why do you think knowing more about God's names, His blessings and all His benefits would help you to trust Him? How and when do you delight in your Heavenly Father?

Our spirit needs to receive the heart of the Father toward us. It includes His kind intentions toward us, His matchless love for us and His glory and kingdom revealed in us. Respond and write down your thoughts:

PRAYER

Record prayer requests and answers to prayer.

PERSONAL NOTES:

6

Lift Up Your Face
To the Father

WORD

Job 22:24-26

26 For then you will have your delight in the Almighty, and lift up your face to God.

Delight in the Almighty

Psalm 37:4

Delight yourself also in the Lord; And He shall give you the desires of your heart.

There are ample opportunities to delight in the Lord and to experience the spiritual joy provided as we engage what heaven is releasing on earth. We have free access to the Father in Christ Jesus our Lord. In whom, because of the blood of Jesus and our faith in Him, we dare to have the boldness, courage and confidence of an unreserved approach to the Father. We can come to Him freely and without fear (see Ephesians 3:11-12).

Coming to the Lord and delighting in Him will cause our

heart's desires to transform. Therefore, He can give us the desires of our heart, because our desires have become His desires for us.

Our devoted relationship with Him should invite extraordinary experiences every day. Do you find your relationship with God missing the power and potential of an unbridled companionship with Him?

Lift up your face to the Father

2 Corinthians 4:6

For it is the God who commanded light to shine out of darkness, who has shone in our hearts to give the light of the knowledge of the glory of God in the face of Jesus Christ.

2 Corinthians 3:18

But we all, with unveiled faces beholding as in a mirror the glory of the Lord, are being transformed into the same image from glory to glory, just as from the Lord, the Spirit.

This scripture explains why Paul prayed the way he did. He knew that the revelations he received from the Lord couldn't be taught, but has to be caught! It's the knowledge of the Father of glory and it's revealed when we encounter Him for ourselves with unveiled faces.

This light is the same light shining in our hearts and it is the knowledge of the glory of God in the face of Jesus Christ. If we only would take time to come closer and to look for it. The glory of God shines in the places where we are becoming who we already are in Christ. It's glorious because it's "filled with all the fullness of Him!" (Ephesians 3:19)

What does it mean to you to lift up your face to the Father?

Awe of God

Hebrews 12:28-29 NIV

28 Therefore, since we are receiving a kingdom that cannot be shaken, let us be thankful, and so worship God acceptably with reverence and awe, 29 for our "God is a consuming fire"

Revelation 4:2-3

2 Behold, a Throne set in heaven, and One sat on the throne. 3 He who sat there was like a jasper and a sardius stone in appearance; and there was a rainbow around the Throne, in appearance like an emerald...

Revelation 21:23

23 The City (New Jerusalem) had no need of the sun or of the moon to shine in it, for the glory of God illuminated it. The Lamb is its light.

If we are truly going to worship God with our lives, it needs to be with reverence and awe recognizing who He truly is.

Awe - a very strong feeling of wonder, reverence, or fear, caused by something grand, magnificent, brilliant or powerful.

Even Apostle John, on the island of Patmos, was in AWE of Jesus Christ when He encountered Him and fell at the feet of Jesus as a dead man.

Revelation 1:17

17 And when I saw Him, I fell at His feet as dead. But He laid His right hand on me, saying to me, "Do not be afraid; I am the First and the Last. 18 I am He who lives, and was dead, and behold, I am alive forevermore. Amen. And I have the keys of Hades and of Death.

It is a blessing to recognize that we can approach our heavenly father with confidence and with closeness, as a child approaches his Daddy (Abba).

At the same time, we need to come closer with a sense of reverence, awe and wonder that we have God Almighty, the Creator of the Universe, the Holy One of Israel, the Great I AM, the Alpha and the Omega, the King of kings and the Lord of lords, as our Heavenly Father.

It is a good idea to avoid our faith becoming so common that we look at God, as we sometimes look at our own fathers, as someone who pays the bills and allows us to borrow the car.

Isaiah 33:17

17 Your eyes will see the King in His beauty...

Psalm 96:6

6 Honor and majesty are before Him; strength and beauty are in His sanctuary.

Song 5:10, 16

10 My Beloved (Jesus) is white (radiant) and ruddy, chief among ten thousand 16 Yes, He is altogether lovely. This is my Beloved, and this is my friend

Desiring to be awestruck by His mysteries and beauty is a need in the core of our being by divine design. There is a craving in every human spirit to be fascinated and loved. We long to be awestruck and filled with endless amazement. Our object or focus of this desire and craving should be the Father, the One we love first.

Have you been amazed and awestruck in the Presence of the Lord?

His eyes are like flames of fire

Revelation 1:14b

...And his eyes were like flames of fire

When the Lord's face shines upon you and me, we can see the glory of God in His face and in the eyes of Jesus we see His fire, we see His passion and we encounter the depth of His love and kind intention toward us.

Speaking to people, we look into their face and more specifically into the eyes. In Matthew 6:22 it states, that the eye is a lamp that provides light for the body. When the eye is good, the whole body is filled with light.

Have you thought about Jesus' eyes being like flames of fire and what that means to you?

PERSONAL APPLICATION

We are encouraged to "come boldly to the throne of grace" Hebrews 4:16. Jesus purchased eternal access for us when the veil was torn in two, removing the separation between the Father and man. What are your thoughts on it?

Jesus face cloth was removed after He was resurrected (see John 20:7), granting access to a face to face connection. Share your thoughts...

PRAYER

Record prayer requests and answers to prayer.

PERSONAL NOTES:

7

Pray to the Father

W O R D

Job 22:27

²⁷ You will make your prayer to Him, and He will hear you, and you will pay your vows.

Pray to the Father

Matthew 6:9-13

In this manner, therefore, pray: Our Father in heaven, Hallowed be Your name. ¹⁰ Your kingdom come. Your will be done on earth as it is in heaven. ¹¹ Give us this day our daily bread. ¹² And forgive us our debts, as we forgive our debtors. ¹³ And do not lead us into temptation, but deliver us from the evil one. For Yours is the kingdom and the power and the glory forever. Amen

When thinking about praying to the Father, I immediately thought of the Lord's Prayer in Matthew 6. Jesus was teaching His disciples a model for prayer and I like to add a few points on how to make this prayer more of an experience with the Father, instead of a recited prayer.

Pointers for Prayer: Pray the Lord's Prayer through, and then take one of the phrases, spending a few moments reflecting on that phrase. For example, imagining what it means for God's Kingdom to come on earth, or how we forgive those who sin against us. Then use these thoughts for further contemplation. Finally coming back to praying through the Lord's Prayer again.

- ➤ Acknowledge Him! By addressing Him as "Our Father in heaven", we acknowledge Who He is: the Almighty, Everlasting One, the Great I Am and He is OUR FATHER!

- ➤ Praise and Adoration! We praise Him and adore Him.

- ➤ Submitting to Him! Alignment with God's kingdom focusing on His magnificence and love.

- ➤ Agreement with His will! His will be done.

- ➤ Asking, Knocking, and Seeking! Daily asking and acknowledgement.

- ➤ Repentance! Asking for forgiveness of any trespasses.

- ➤ Forgiveness! Forgiving others.

- ➤ Divine Guidance! Asking for wisdom, knowledge and understanding for daily living.

- ➤ Protection and Peace!

- ➤ Worship, Exaltation and Thanksgiving!

Can you share about your prayer life, what would you like to be different?

Priest and King

Revelation 1:5-6

5 and from Jesus Christ, the faithful witness, the firstborn from the dead, and the ruler over the kings of the earth. To Him who loved us and washed us from our sins in His own blood, 6 and has made us kings and priests to His God and Father, to Him be glory and dominion forever and ever. Amen.

In above scripture we are called kings and priests. As a priest we stand in the Presence of God to worship and pray to Him. As a king we intercede, declare and decree the Word and insight we heard from God, while worshipping and spending precious time with Him. He gives us the spirit of wisdom and revelation in the knowledge of Him and all mysteries hidden in Jesus Christ.

It is an honor to pray a "Prayer of Consecration" to invite the Lord to work deep within our hearts. So that Jesus might be seen in greater ways through our lives.

Intercession

In 1 John 2:1 AMP, Jesus is our Advocate, who is interceding for us. Interceding means someone stands in the gap and pleads (court room language) a case for another.

Focus on Intercession:

Ezekiel 22:30
So I sought for a man among them who would make a wall, and stand in the gap before Me on behalf of the land, that I should not destroy it; but I found no one.

Romans 8:34
Who is he who condemns? It is Christ who died, and furthermore is also risen, who is even at the right hand of God, who also makes intercession for us.

Following are some impulses:

Pray for nations and cities
Psalm 22:27-28, Psalm 127:1, Matthew 9:35-37

Pray for a spiritual awakening among the lost
2 Peter 3:9, John 14:13-14, 16:24

Pray for God-given dreams and visions
Joel 2:28-29

Pray for leaders
Ephesians 4:11, 1 Timothy 2:1-3

Pray for God to send his workers from every nation into the harvest field of the world
Matthew 9:37-38, Matthew 28:19-20

Pray for the body of Christ to reach out to those who are poor and needy
Proverbs 21:13, Hebrews 13:3

Declare/Decree

Job 22:28

You will also declare a thing, And it will be established for you; So light will shine on your ways.

Let's remember who we are in Christ! We are His ambassadors and we live in this world, but are not off this world, because our citizenship is in Heaven. Since we are born again of the Spirit of God, we can see His kingdom and the kingdom is within us. Therefore, we have the authority to release kingdom manifestations, such as healing, deliverance, salvation, miracles, signs and wonders.

As new covenant believers, we have been given access to the throne of grace, and have been told we can come boldly before that third heaven throne room to obtain mercy and grace (Hebrews 4:16).

We also are shown things to come and the Lord will give us scriptures, we can declare over situations, nations, regions and cities. For instance:

Esther was standing in the gap for her people, the Jews, because she was called for such a time. She was given favor by the king and he told her: "you yourself write a decree concerning the Jews as you please, in the king's name and seal it with the king's signet ring (see Esther 8:8).

God's hand of providence and protection on behalf of His people is evident throughout the Book of Esther. Haman's plot brings great danger to the Jews and is countered by the courage of Esther and her wise cousin and counselor Mordecai, resulting in a great deliverance because of the decree. She was granted to write the decree in the king's name and it was sealed with the king's signet ring, therefore no one can revoke it.

We can pray to the Father in the name of Jesus and whatever we ask we receive from Him, because we keep His commandments and do those things that are pleasing in His sight (1 John 3:22). Esther was concerned not just about herself, but she did what was pleasing in God's sight. Therefore, we can decree and declare the Lord's will. (Read the Book of Esther)

King David prayed:

1 Chronicles 17:23-24a

And now, O Lord, the word which You have spoken concerning Your servant and concerning his house, let it be established forever, and do as You have said. So let it be established, that Your name may be magnified forever.

Here an example on how we can declare a thing:

Declaring according to 1 Thessalonians 5:4-10*: As believers, we are sons of the light and sons of the day. We are wide awake and clothed in the armor of light. The Holy Spirit is training us to be alert, watchful and on our guard as we walk in Him.*

Job prepared his case and knew he was going to be vindicated. (Job 13:18). Any thoughts on this in light of "declaring/decreeing a thing"?

PERSONAL APPLICATION

Are you prepared to proclaim the promises of the Lord over your life, family, work and city? What are your declarations?

DECLARATION

We declare that the word which You, Lord, has spoken concerning Your servant and concerning His house will be established forever. Let it be established, that Your name may be magnified forever.

We declare that every aspect of our life will yield abundant fruit for the glory of God.

PERSONAL NOTES:

DELIGHT IN THE FATHER OF GLORY

DELIGHT ~

TO LOVE SOMEONE GREATLY; TO BE FASCINATED, CAPTIVATED AND ATTRACTED

ABOUT THE AUTHOR

Gabriele Gilpin, an ordained minister and graduate of Rhema Bible School, is the President and Founder of Soaring Eagle Ministries, Inc.

During her 25+ years of ministry, she has also served as an apostolic lighthouse leader and overseer, traveling preacher, teacher, conference speaker, translator, missionary and author.

Her vision is international and a part of building the Kingdom of God. The vision includes equipping, training and releasing the saints, to do the work of ministering toward building up Christ's body according to Ephesians 4:12, and to truly "soar on wings as eagles." Many have been transformed by the demonstration of the power of God and His Word.

She has been passionate about developing leadership internationally and has been on television, radio and is hosting an internet radio show. Gabriele has seen numerous salvations, miracles, healings, deliverances, signs and wonders following the preaching of the Word. God's anointing on this ministry has been instrumental in helping many individuals to stir up and release the God-given gifts within them in order to start walking in God's calling and purposes for their lives. The preaching, teaching and prayer ministry releases the fire of the Holy Spirit and a prophetic voice to the hearer.

Gabriele served in Aglow International for nearly 15 years starting in 1991 and was president of Aglow lighthouses in New Jersey, and Florida. She pioneered and started the Aglow lighthouse in Hillsborough, New Jersey, as well as serving on the Northeast Florida Area Team of Aglow International.

Presently, both she and her husband are living in Florida.

For speaking engagements, Rev. Gabriele Gilpin can be contacted by email, phone or the website.

For more information, to partner with us, or to be added to the mailing list, please contact us:

Soaring Eagle Ministries, Inc.
10990 Ft. Caroline Road # 350352,
Jacksonville, FL 32225

Website:
www.soaringeagleinc.org

Email:
info@soaringeagleinc.org

Follow the Blog:

www.soaringeagleinc.org/blog

Like us on the Facebook Page:

https://www.facebook.com/SoaringEagleMinistries

Or listen to
Teaching on Internet Radio Talk Shoe
http://www.talkshoe.com/tc/118015

Life Transforming Resources from Soaring Eagle Ministries:

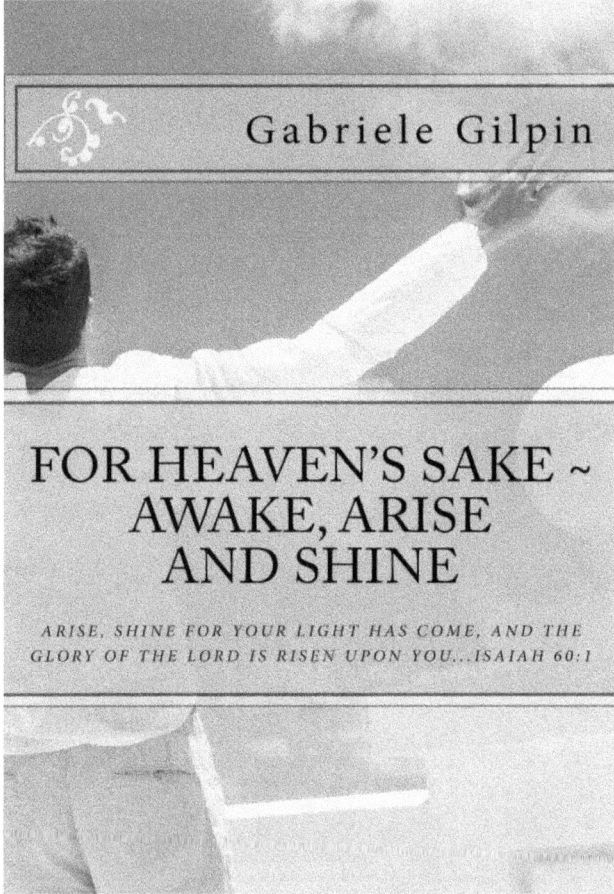

Gabriele Gilpin

FOR HEAVEN'S SAKE ~ AWAKE, ARISE AND SHINE

ARISE, SHINE FOR YOUR LIGHT HAS COME, AND THE GLORY OF THE LORD IS RISEN UPON YOU...ISAIAH 60:1

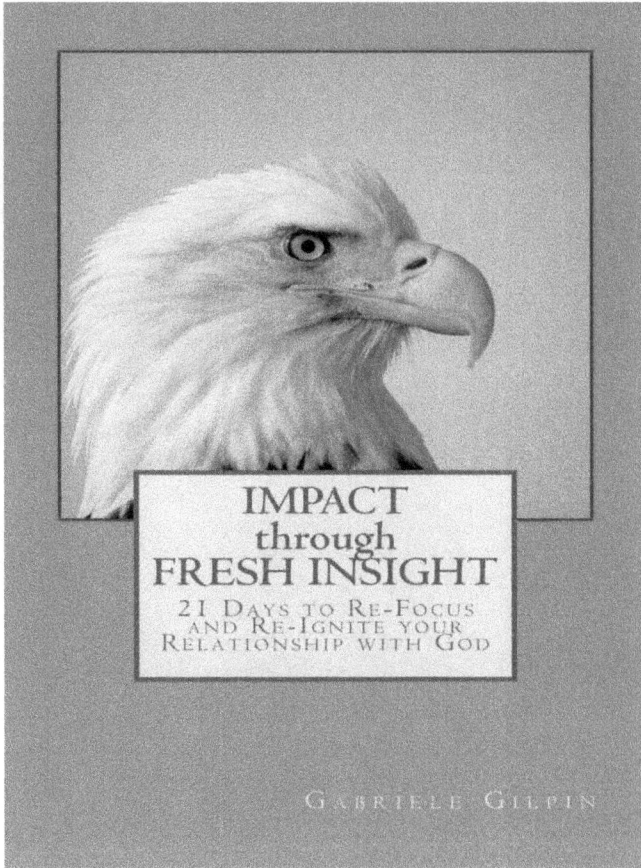

If interested obtain prices and order online on our website or on Amazon.com:

www.amazon.com/GabrieleGilpin
www.soaringeagleinc.org/contactandsupport.html

www.ingramcontent.com/pod-product-compliance
Lightning Source LLC
Chambersburg PA
CBHW060040040426
42331CB00032B/1871